JonBenet Ramsey

The Murder Mystery That Shocked America

Frances J. Armstrong

Introduction

JonBenet Ramsey, a name that is still known in every household across the USA - starting in 1996 and now burned in the minds of everyone over the last 20 years.

And yet, no one knows who killed her.

It destroyed the lives of the family, lives in the community, destroyed friendships, hurt the town of Boulder, and made media with all their lies and leaky news stories nothing but a circus.

It is the fear every parent holds in their heart about their children. No matter how much you protect your child, it seems it is never enough.

Evil seems to lurk at every corner and sometimes in your own home in the basement.

JonBenet Ramsey in the Beginning...

JonBenet Patricia Ramsey was born August 6, 1990, at 1:36 a.m. in Atlanta, Georgia, U.S.A.

She was born into the world of high society thanks to her mother, Patricia Ann Paugh Ramsey (her birth 12/29/56) and her very wealthy father who was a businessman John Bennett Ramsey (his birth 12/7/87). John was the President and founder of Access Graphics, which was a computer systems company that later became connected as a subsidiary of Lockheed Martin.

JonBenet was named after her father and had one older brother by the name of Burke, who was at the time of her birth three years older.

She also had two half-siblings, John Andrew and Melinda.

John Ramsey had been married previously to Lucinda Pasch for twelve years. They had three children in this marriage. They were Elizabeth Pasch Ramsey, Melinda Ramsey, and John Andrew Ramsey.

John Ramsey lost two children in the 1990's, more than any father should have to bear. Elizabeth (Beth) Ramsey worked as an airline stewardess. She was with her then boyfriend, Matt Derrington, also age 22, when the BMW they were in collided with a bakery truck near the city of Chicago during inclement weather. Both Matt and Beth died. Beth was found to have died of enormous internal injuries.

JonBenet lived a happy five-year old's life it seemed in their families 15-room home in Boulder, Colorado.

Or, was she? After all, her mother had been a beauty queen when she was younger and fought for her beauty titles. But, with age, the beauty had faded, and with ovarian cancer, the aging process was hastening faster for Patsy Ramsey. It seemed she was living vicariously through her little girl.

JonBenet was beautiful, even without all the makeup, the false eyelashes, the extra hairpieces, the fake teeth, the sprayed-on suntan, the thick, thick makeup, the thousands of dollars of clothes and costumes as well as all the trainers and coaches she had to win the contests. Patsy was determined to make sure Jon Benet would win.

With all the pageants, all the coaching and training, the hours in the salons, all the trips required to attend the trainings and fittings for dresses, when did JonBenet have time just to be a little girl?

She won many titles in her competitions. Among them was America's Tiny Little Miss, America's Royale Miss, Little Miss Colorado, Little Miss Charlevoix, Colorado State All-Star Kids Cover-Girl, and National Tiny Miss.

Christmas night, 1996, JonBenet would face her most fierce competition she had ever encountered, and unfortunately, it would be one she would lose.

It Had Been A Beautiful Christmas

The Ramseys had their usual Christmas that morning. They all went downstairs around six in the morning to open presents which took them all about an hour.

After the gift opening, John and Patsy went into the kitchen to make the traditional Christmas breakfast they always made for the kids, and that included pancakes. JonBenet was running around wanting to help John make the pancakes like always; wanting to pour the batter into Mickey Mouse shaped heads so she could decorate it on her plate.

After breakfast, the kids went back to playing with their toys and neighborhood kids were coming by to see what Santa left for Burke and JonBenet. So, there were lots of kids in and out of the house all morning long.

Patsy stayed busy packing for their trip to Michigan to visit friends there and to stay for a while in their vacation home and then on to a Disney cruise with the kids. At some point that morning, John went to the hangar to check on their airplane.

That evening they all went to the White's for Christmas Dinner as they had the year before. After leaving the Whites, they dropped off a gift at the Stines and Walker's homes. By the time they finally got to their house, JonBenet was asleep, so John carried her up to her room from the car.

Patsy pulled the covers back, John laid her down, and Patsy got her partially undressed and then tried to find some pajama bottoms but was unsuccessful, so she put some long underwear pants on her instead.

Burke, being all excited about a model garage he had gotten for Christmas didn't want to go to sleep until he finished putting it together, so John helped him finish it up so they could all get to bed and get some rest for tomorrow. So, Burke went on to his room as did Patsy and John to their room.

The next morning, Burke, who was nine years old at the time, can remember hearing his mother running around and screaming downstairs when he awoke. He can remember thinking that whatever is going on it did not sound like they were going to be going on their Disney Cruise.

What had happened he was to find out later was when his mom, Patsy awoke the day after Christmas and she could not find JonBenet, she was frantically searching the house for her.

Patsy called the police at around 5:52 a.m. She was screaming for them to send help because her little girl was missing and someone had left a long ransom note on their back staircase.

As a matter of fact, the ransom note was 2 ½ pages in length, and the kidnapper was telling them they must come up with $118,000. The printing in the note was block style, had precise margins, it made a reference to the Philippines at a Navy Air Base where John had served one time. They noticed the note had four words misspelled that looked like they were being done so intentionally.

The police arrived within three minutes, and they made a quick search of the house. Two more hours went by, and a detective came, with FBI agents showing up at 10:30 a.m.

It was 1:00 p.m. before anyone in the group thought about looking in the basement, and that is when John Ramsey found his daughter's dead body.

John Ramsey saw that there was a rope tied around her neck and a stick that the cord was wrapped around. Part of her ponytail had been caught up in the rope placed around her neck, JonBenet was on her back, covered by a blanket and sweatshirt, duct tape covered her mouth, her little head turning to her right, and her arms were above her head. She had on a white long-sleeved knit shirt with no collar, and a silver star on it covered with sequins.

She had on long white underwear with urine and red stains on her panties.

There was a heart drawn in the palm of her left hand with a red ink pen and a gold cross necklace dangled from her neck. She had on a gold bracelet with her name on it and the date of 12-25-96 engraved along with a ring on her right finger.

For some reason, John Ramsey removed the tape that was covering her mouth and carried her body upstairs where everyone had gathered.

By the time John Ramsey found her little body, it was already in rigor mortis indicating that she had to have died sometime between 10:00 p.m. Christmas night and 6:00 a.m. December 26th.

John laid her little body down upstairs and later, Arndt moved her into the living room by the Christmas tree, and there it stayed until that night at 10:45 when the staff from the morgue took her away.

Burke, Patsy, and John all gave blood, hair and handwriting samples to the police.

Patsy and John did participate in an interview that lasted for more than two hours, and a couple of weeks later it was Burke's turn.

At the funeral home, JonBenet laying in such sweet repose was wearing one of her pageant gowns and a tiara. Patsy's mother had a unique bracelet she was going to give to JonBenet when she was older, but she reached down and placed it on Jon Benet's wrist in the coffin.

Polly, Patsy's sister, put a gold cross in JonBenet's hands. While Patsy was suffering from her ovarian cancer, Father Rol had a healing service for Patsy and gave her a cross which had received blessings of Native Americans living in South Dakota where he had pastored at one time.

Patsy later found similar gold crosses in a store in Boulder and bought one for each of her sisters and her mother. Polly, who had gone through some difficult times herself, had worn her cross, JonBenet would have it forever in eternity.

Pam is the one who brought in JonBenet's Little Miss Christmas Tiara and placed it so lovingly on JonBenet's tiny head.

John had recently bought a silk scarf, and he tucked around little JonBenet like he was trying to surround her with his blanket of love.

Priscilla White rushed into the funeral home. Priscilla and Fleet, Ramsey's neighbors, had located Sister Socks, a little-stuffed kitten that was one of JonBenet's favorites. Patsy placed it under JonBenet's right arm.

Burke's main memory of his sister's funeral was that her casket was so very tiny.

Following her funeral service, JonBenet's interment was in Marietta, Georgia next to her much older half-sister who had died in a car wreck.

About six months after JonBenet's death, John and Patsy left Boulder, Colorado and moved to Atlanta, Georgia and never returned to Boulder.

Evidence to be Considered

One of the first things that make you sit up and say, this just does not feel right, is the odd ransom note. But before delving into the note let me make mention of a couple of issues to think about as we go over this famous piece of evidence.

First and foremost, you will not usually find ransom notes that are 2 ½ pages long. Secondly, the ransom demand was for almost the exact dollar amount John Ramsey's latest bonus was at work.

Third, the ransom note had been written at the crime scene on a notepad at the Ramsey home. Fourth, they had written a practice 'note' before writing the 'real' one. Fifth, there were no fingerprints to be found on the letter.

And last but not least, the handwriting expert that evaluated the note says it matches exactly with Patsy Ramsey's handwriting samples. Patsy makes her printed A's in four different ways, and within the Ransom note, all various methods of the A's are visible. Please notice the spelling errors that are in the letter that looks intentional.

Now, for the ransom note, I will quote it verbatim from the detective's files now available online:

Mr. Ramsey,

Listen carefully! We are a group of individuals that represent a small foreign faction. We do respect your bussiness [sic] but not the country that it serves. At this time we have your daughter in our posession[sic]. She is safe and unharmed, and if you want her to see 1997, you must follow our instructions to the letter.

You will withdraw $118,000 from your account. $100,000 will be in $100 bills and the remaining $18,000 will be $20 bills. Make sure that you bring an adequate size attache to the bank. When you get home you will put the money in a brown paper bag. I will call you between 8, and 10 am tomorrow to instruct you on delivery. The delivery will be exhausting, so I advise you to be rested. If we monitor you getting the money early, we might call you early to arrange an earlier delivery of the money and hence a [sic] earlier ~~delivery~~ of your daughter.

Any deviation from any instructions will result in the immediate execution of your daughter. You will also be denied her remains for proper burial. The two gentlemen watching over your daughter do particularly like you, so I do advise you not to provoke them. Speaking to anyone about your situation such as Police, FBI, etc., will result in your daughter being beheaded. If we catch you talking to a stray dog, she dies. If you *alert bank authorities, she dies. If the money is in any way marked or tampered with, she dies. You will be scanned for electronic devices, and if any are found, she dies. You can try to deceive us but be warned that we are familiar with law enforcement countermeasures and tactics. You stand a 99% chance of killing your daughter if you try to out smart [sic] us. Follow our instructions, and you stand a 100% chance of getting her back.*

You and your family are under constant scrutiny as well as the authorities. Don't try to grow a brain, John. You are not the only fat cat around so don't think that killing will be difficult. Don't underestimate us, John. Use that good southern common sense of yours. It is up to you now John!

Victory!

S.B.T.C.

Thinking that JonBenet's bedroom was the origin of the crime scene, so it was the only room in the house cordoned off so it would not become contaminated.

There were so many friends and then the family's minister came to the house to support Pat and John. Victim advocacy representatives arrived on the scene, and everyone was picking up and cleaning stuff around the house and kitchen and probably destroying evidence as they 'helped.'

About 8:00 a.m., Linda Arndt, a detective from Boulder police force showed up on the scene to wait for instructions of the kidnapper(s) as to the next steps for the money drop. There was no such contact.

The following are evidence statements made by the Ramseys former housekeeper, Linda Hoffman-Pugh:

- A Swiss Arm Knife found in the same basement room where John Benet's dead body lay.

- The only person who could have placed that army knife there was Patsy. Hoffman-Pugh said that she had taken it away from Burke and then hid it in the linen closet outside JohnBenet's bedroom. No intruder would not have been able to find it. Patsy would have been the only one to find it when she got out clean sheets.

- The blanket that had been used to wrap around JonBenet's body had to come from the dryer. This blanket still had a Barbie doll nightgown clinging to it, meaning it had to come out of the dryer just recently. The only person who would have known it was in the dryer would have been Patsy.

- An intruder would never have been able to locate the room in the basement, let alone the door leading to it where they discovered Jon Benet's body.

- The housekeeper testified that Patsy had become moody before Christmas that year. It seemed to her like Patsy had multiple personalities. One minute she would be in a good mood, and then the next minutes she would be cranky all over again.

- Patsy was getting into disagreements with JonBenet about wearing different clothes or a dress or a friend coming over. The housekeeper said she had never seen Patsy acting like this.

- Given to the Grand Jury was the analysis of six handwriting experts of Patsy Ramsey's writing and copies of the ransom note. All six of the jurors felt it very likely that she, Patsy was the one who wrote that ransom note.

- No identification ever for the boot print and a palm print near her body.

- No link to anyone from DNA found under JonBenet's fingernails.

- There was one door unlocked that night, a window down in the basement was opened, and the house's alarm system was not on.

- No signs of forced entry anywhere.

- No footprints in the snow ANYWHERE outside the house.

- When John Ramsey was asked to search the home, he automatically started in the basement.

- Odd that the ransom demand was the same amount of John Ramsey's bonus.

- As wealthy as the Ramsey's were, the kidnapper could have asked for millions if it had been a real criminal.

- The Ramsey's kept all their friends and family members from talking to the police.

- The weird 911 call by Patsy seemed very strange. When Patsy had thought she had hung up the phone but had not you can hear John Ramsey's voice saying 'we are not speaking to you' and then Patsy's voice 'help me, Jesus, what did you do?' and then a younger voice that is saying 'what did you find?'.

- During police interviews, Patsy and John were combative and tried to throw all suspicion away from themselves.

- Patsy had on the same clothes that she wore to the White's Christmas party the night before.

- JonBenet suffered from severe but blunt force trauma to the back of her head, and on top of that, she suffered from strangulation. A rope was used to strangle her, and a paint brush of Patsy's had been fashioned as a garrote to tighten the cord.

- JonBenet apparently was hit on the back of her head with something round with a flat type top. Detectives think a flashlight would be most likely.

- During the autopsy, contents of her stomach revealed she had eaten pineapple before she died. It meant she had to have eaten something after coming home and her parents said she had not eaten anything after coming back to their house. The only fingerprints on the bowl were those of her brother Burke.

- The Ramsey's had their own personal Santa that JonBenet worshiped. She thought he was the real deal. He was Bill McReynolds who was living out his retirement from being a journalism professor. Supposedly he gave JonBenet a note that told her something special was going to happen to her after Christmas. And to top off the weirdness, the professor's wife had supposedly written a screenplay before JonBenet's murder about a little girl that was tortured and then murdered in her basement.

- Before the Ramsey's would even sit down for an interview with the Boulder police, they went on national TV on CNN and to talk to the world. Body language experts feel that they were not genuine, it was all rehearsed, and everything felt forced.

- The mystery figure in all of this is nine-year-old Burke, JonBenet's brother.

- One of Patsy's friends was later talking to police and fingered Burke for the murder. The friend said that after JonBenet got involved in pageants that Burke was very jealous. She said that Burke would have violent outbursts. One time he gave JonBenet a black eye by hitting her with a golf club.

- When the Ramseys interview time came they were interviewed separately; months had passed. Their stories matched identically. Like they had been coached and rehearsed over and over again.

- Back to the ransom note, we find that the handwriting matches Patsy's almost to a T.

- The initial reports claimed there had been no signs of forced entry; there was a damaged basement window that was later investigated as a potential point of entry. Detective Kolar grew frustrated with the intruder theory because of one small, but a possibly significant piece of evidence. There was a little triangle of cobwebs in the window that had not been disturbed, and no one could have gotten through that small window without knocking down that cobweb.

- There was also a shared of glass from the broken window lying on the window sill, and that would have probably been raked away if someone had tried to enter.

- Experts from CBS reported that several of the lines in the ransom note were from movies, inclusive of Dirty Harry and Speed.

- The Ramsey family's home supposedly was not supposed to be in the nicest neighborhood. There were reports of over 100 burglaries in this area in the months before JonBenet's death. This community had a high concentration of creepy people, with 38 registered sex offenders that lived within two miles of the Ramseys house at the time of Jon Benet's death.

- The fact that it was in a bad neighborhood is extremely hard to buy since all the homes in the neighborhood were all so expensive. That just does not hold water when you look at it.

A Few Theories

<u>The Steve Thomas Theory</u>- Steve was one of the lead detectives in the case at the beginning. He thinks that Patsy went in a "bed-wetting-rage." He felt that Patsy never did go to bed that night, but wound up killing JonBenet and worked the rest of the night covering up a crime she had committed.

He feels this is evidenced by the fact that Patsy was still wearing the same clothes she had on the evening before at the White's party.

He adds that Patsy is the one who wrote the ransom letter to make it look like an intruder came in and kidnapped JonBenet.

He also felt that sometime during the night, JonBenet got up after wetting the bed, and this made Patsy so mad that she flew into a rage. She and JonBenet had an 'encounter' in the bathroom, and that is when Patsy slammed JonBenet's head into a hard surface, causing the most terrible, but deadly head wound.

His speculation goes on with the thought process that at this point, Patsy thought that JonBenet was dead, but yet could still feel her heart beating and needed to do something to finish her off. He feels that is why she chose to strangle her to death with the garrote to make sure she was dead.

You could make defense here that she was setting the scene to make it look like an intruder. But with the head wound so severe, there were no visible signs of it on the outside, so Patsy could not tell that in fact that there was an 8 inch long crack in the skull and the fact was a huge piece of skull pushed forward into the brain, and the brain was bleeding.

While John and Burke Ramsey were still sleeping upstairs, and with JonBenet only weighing 48 pounds, Patsy gets her body down to the basement. Goes back upstairs to make up the crazy ransom note and then back downstairs to 'stage' the kidnapper/murder scene.

Instead of being happy that her daughter was still alive and calling for help, she decided to finish her off and plan this elaborate scheme.

Mr. Thomas also feels that after Mr. Ramsey read that ransom note the next morning is when he got suspicious. It is at this point where John Ramsey probably decided to protect his wife.

Darnay Hoffman – he felt that Patsy killed JonBenet with a blow to her head in a fit of rage just because Patsy was not happy, suffering from depression and that she and John Ramsey were having marital problems.

While Patsy was dealing with her ovarian cancer for two years, John Ramsey was said to have had an affair with another woman.

The Globe's story contends that JonBenet died from a fight when Patsy walked in on John and JonBenet during one of John's weird sex games with his daughter. Maybe Patsy woke up during the middle of the night and heard some funny noises in the early morning hours and realized John was not in their bed.

Patsy grabbed a mag flashlight and headed in the direction of the sound and found her husband strangling their daughter during a sick sex game leading to a ferocious fight and Patsy hit the wrong person with the flashlight.

Dale Yeager was asked by Boulder Police Department to analyze the ransom letter, and he made a public statement that said Patsy was a sociopath who not only abused her daughter but was the one who killed her.

Dr. Morris stated that Patsy had Munchausen-by-Proxy Syndrome. Patsy herself a former beauty queen craved attention and was willing to do anything to get it. In three years time, she had JonBenet to the pediatrician 27 times. Face it; the case ended when Pasty died, or at least for 20 years until it came back to life again.

Some people think that Patsy is knowing or unknowingly involved JonBenet in some child pornography ring. Even the original photographer who did all of her pictures stated his life was over after her murder and was thought to be a possible murder suspect.

The Boulder Police Department asked for a psychological profile done of Patsy Ramsey. The report of that profile concludes that she was a delusional sociopath. It is with religious sociopaths; she saw herself with JonBenet's death for it to be like a sacrifice for her 'sins.'

The crime itself was committed by a sociopath that was delusional and had herself convinced that she was innocent. People that are sociopaths never see themselves as being guilty of any wrongdoing.

Mark Soukap has a theory that Patsy killed JonBenet intentionally. She did this for Patsy as part of her sick psychotic fantasy that had some craziness around a supernatural being. She feared judgment by God and fearing death.

She did not want to kill JonBenet, but just to make an angel out of her. Right after the funeral, Patsy said JonBenet is in heaven waiting for my arrival, and it won't be long. Patsy was nuts and was putting JonBenet in heaven to assure that she would be in eternity when she arrived.

What some do not understand is that what they think is staging is that the ligatures were suspension devices so Patsy could view her body and then take it down and do all the rest she had planned on doing to the child.

The incriminating evidence regarding Patsy. More child abuse happens over toilet training than any other developmental time in their life.

Head trauma is the leading cause of death in child abuse.

Strangling children to death is not uncommon for a mother. There was one mother who killed all four of her children by strangulation.

Dale Yeager developed a report for the Boulder Police Department. In it, there were these assertions.

The individual who killed JonBenet had no experience in the murder of a human.

Blunt trauma to the skull and then strangulation did so because they were frustrated. The first method failed, so the murderer had to resort to another method to get the job done. All the bruising may have come from struggling with the child before her death.

Based on previous experience, the crime was committed by someone who was intimate with and had an emotional attachment to the deceased.

Fiber Evidence – red fibers from Patsy's red sweater she had worn the night before to the White's Christmas party were in the paint brush caddy Patsy used. There were also red fibers on the blanket around JonBenet's body, on the Duct tape on the sticky side, and tied up in the knots of the ligature that had been used to strangle JonBenet.

Patsy's side of the bed had not been slept in that night.

The ten different handwriting experts who reviewed the ransom note all came to the same conclusion without knowing what the other experts had concluded. The result was that Patsy Ramsey had written the Ransom letter.

The Ramseys were so careful to hide behind their lawyers. Most parents of kidnapped children are going to be out crusading trying to get their kids back.

John and Patsy kept avoiding the police like they were the plague. They used lawyers that were national high powered guys and public relation personnel.

You would think that they would be at the police station every day, but instead, they headed to Atlanta.

When the Boulder police would confront her with damning evidence that made her look guilty she was always evasive with an answer.

Her sister Pam Paugh knew what was going on as well. She helped remove evidence. After John and Patsy had left the Boulder house, Patsy had her sister Pam go back to pick up funeral clothing.

Pam picked up much more than that. The rest of the duct tape and the cord that were part of a painting had to be taken by Pam, and that explains the 'missing' items that the Boulder Police could not find.

Placing the ransom note on the back staircase raises questions. How would the kidnapper know to place the ransom letter on that staircase?

Expert opinion on the 'accidental' head blow states that the fractures of the skull revelation let you know it was more likely from high-force trauma. If it is depressed and wider than 3 cm, is multiple, or if it crosses a suture line or the base of the skull.'

A quick lesson. 3 mm is 0.1 inches. JonBenet's fracture was a ½ inch wide at the portion where the skull had been 'punched out,' and pushing into the brain, making it bleed.

With the hole in the head being the size it was, there was no way a fall caused it.

Cord fibers were in JonBenet's bed. The same threads that came from the garrote around JonBenet's throat.

Some feel that this crime was too horrible for a parent to commit.

To sexually assault your child after they are at death's door is such a terrible act in and of itself.

The autopsy did reveal that JonBenet suffered from 'chronic' sexual abuse. In profiling, they ruled out John Ramsey since he had had an affair with another woman while Patsy was going through cancer treatment for ovarian cancer and he had cheated on his first wife.

In searching all of his computers, there was nothing that connected him to desire children.

Who would have been the chronic abuser?

It is 2003 – The Ramseys Fight Back

It is seven years later, and there have been no new developments. No new leads into finding the killer for JonBenet's.

It didn't matter, the Ramsey's were on the offensive, and they were spending money to prove their innocence. They launched a massive and costly public relations campaign, and this included their book, 'The Death of Innocence,' in which they made sure to exonerate themselves and their son Burke of the murder.

In the book, it did speculate regarding who it might be, and it included dozens of their close friends, trusted household workers, Santa's wife, the man who had played Santa for the Ramsey's the last three years, and former business colleagues.

It is impossible to imagine what their close friends felt at this point. There was one friend, a very close friend of theirs for a very long time as a matter of fact. That was Fleet White.

It is the talk that after the funeral in Atlanta that Fleet had told John Ramsey, that the next time he saw John, he wanted it to be in a courtroom. In the early parts of the investigation into JonBenet's death, Fleet kept writing open letters to all the people who lived in Boulder.

He wanted them to join with him in calling for the appointment of a special prosecutor to JonBenet's case. He felt that the current attorney might be in a compromising position because of the Ramseys and that the police of Boulder were getting a bum rap.

Fleet White had gone to serve as a pallbearer for JonBenet in Atlanta, and he found out that the Ramseys had no intention of returning to Boulder to help police, and this made him angry.

Fleet's wife had never agreed with Patsy putting JonBenet into the pageants and all that she put the little girl through. She even bought Patsy a book that addressed what putting children in pageants at this age could do to them in later years. Patsy did not even listen to her. Patsy was going to do what she wanted. Fleet and his wife felt sorry for JonBenet. She didn't have time to be a child.

The Ramseys promoted their website (www.ramseyfamily.com) where it offered $100,000 for a reward for information that would lead them to JonBenet's killer arrest and conviction.

In August of 2000, Patsy got even bolder by taking on the Boulder police department with a top, front page headline in the newspaper USA Today. It said that "If you think I am the one who did it, let's go to trial and get this mess over with."

She and John were just tired and wanted some normalcy in their lives. They were tired and frustrated and wanted the circus to end.

They agreed to interviews for a day and a half in Atlanta by the Boulder District Attorney's office.

Then the Ramseys were again asked to take a polygraph test. They agreed but with three conditions:

- It had to be done independently from the Boulder Police Department

- It must be in Atlanta

- The results had to be made public

Things were going good, so the Boulder Police set up to have the FBI specialists handle the polygraph examinations. They said that FBI polygraphers would be independent of Boulder and they had the international recognition of lie detector testing.

The Ramseys wanted to get the lie detector testing over with because they knew it would establish their innocence. It would deliver them home free to all the public opinion and probably to any of the Colorado prosecutors on down the road.

Ramsey's attorney, however, told the Boulder police that they were reluctant on taking an exam conducted by the FBI since the FBI had previously been involved in the murder investigation and would keep them from being true 'independent' examiners.

To try and compromise, the FBI then agreed to get an examiner that had no prior knowledge and never worked on JonBenet's case, and the Boulder police decided they would not get involved in selecting who the FBI examiners.

The offer caused a stalemate because it just did not satisfy what the Ramseys had wanted and it did not meet their concerns regarding the FBI. The Boulder Police Department would not budge on the compromise either. The lie detector tests went dead in their tracks.

Chief Beckner from Boulder said that he was disappointed that the Ramseys had declined to take the offered lie detector testing after announcing that they would. If they ever changed their minds, to just let him know.

The Ramseys started to think maybe this would make them look bad, so they regrouped with their attorney. During May 6 through 17, they succumbed to 'a series' of lie detector tests given to them by prominent national polygraphers of their choosing.

A news conference held by their attorney announcing that they had passed the lie detector tests and Patsy Ramsey said she 'felt great about the results.'

Police Chief Becker said the whole thing was nothing but a media circus, a publicity campaign.

In 2000, Governor of Colorado, Bill Owens told reporters that based on all the evidence, the Ramseys still needed to be held under an umbrella of suspicion.

A chief detective in the case, Steve Thomas, resigned from the Boulder Police Department when he found out that the investigators who knew about the situation better than anyone else that they would not be getting involved as grand jury advisory witnesses.

Thomas formed a letter that showed what a deep chasm existed between the Boulder Police and the Prosecutor's office. He said this gap along with the Ramseys, not cooperating with the investigation has done nothing but shielded a murderer.

Thomas goes on to write a book by the name of *JonBenet, Inside the Ramsey Murder Investigation.* Inside the book, you will find that he names Patsy Ramsey is the one who murdered her daughter.

Nearly ten years pass and the tragedy boils up again when John Mark Karr, some teacher living in Thailand made the claim that he was JonBenet's killer. He said it was just an accident that resulted from a weird sexual encounter they had. He claimed he had given her drugs.

Karr was so stupid. None of what he had said even happened. DNA tests soon proved that he was nowhere near Ramsey's home, there were no drugs in JonBenet's system, Karr was in Georgia when the murder occurred which made all of it impossible.

Investigator Thomas Has Theories

We have touched briefly on Thomas's theories, but this time, we will go a little deeper as his ideas make so much more sense.

Thomas felt that Patsy who was approaching the big 40 and a busy holiday season, and after a very tiring Christmas Day, she had maybe a couple of glasses of wine, and then got into an argument with JonBenet.

Patsy was upset that her beautiful little girl that she always tried to dress up like her twin was starting to rebel against her by wanting to wear different clothes than what Patsy wore. Patsy liked for her and JonBenet to always dress like twins.

At home from the Whites', John was helping Burke put together that Christmas toy and JonBenet, who probably had not eaten much at the Whites' party was hungry. Patsy gave her some pineapple, and they put the kids to bed. John read to JonBenet and then he went on to bed. Patsy was up a while getting ready for the trip the next day, one she did not want to make.

JonBenet woke up later after wetting her bed, which was noticeable by the plastic sheets, the pull-up diapers that were hanging out of the cabinet and urine stains, as well as a balled up turtleneck found in JonBenet's bathroom. It looked like JonBenet had put on the red turtleneck to wear to bed, and removed when it got wet.

Thomas said he never felt JonBenet suffered the sexual abuse for the gratification of the offender; instead, it seemed it was some form of horrible punishment. The dark fibers in her pubic area could have come from some wiping off a child who was wet.

Thomas believes that JonBenet was slammed up against a hard surface, like the edge of a sink or tub causing the mortal head wound.

She would have been unconscious, but her heart would have still been beating, and Patsy would have thought she was still alive and might wake up and tell someone what happened.

So here Patsy was faced with the decision of whether to call an ambulance or figure out an explanation of why her daughter was in this shape.

An emergency room doctor would have been suspicious of an injury like this and called the police. Probably little would have happened to Patsy Ramsey in Boulder, but panic set in and she acted irrationally.

Burke and John were still sleeping, and Patsy took JonBenet down to the basement into that little room.

As Thomas figures, Patsy's dilemma was that the police might assume the obvious if a six-year-old was found dead in her home for no real reason. Patsy had to think of a scheme as to why she was dead and how a kidnapping should look.

Thomas believes that Patsy being so rattled at this point that she went upstairs to the kitchen to try and write a ransom letter, and used one of their tablets and a felt tip pen they had in a drawer or on the counter. She opened the tablet up to the middle and started to write a ransom note.

But, for some reason, Patsy did not like it and ripped those pages out and got rid of them, but the police searched for them, and they were not able to find them. Then at some point, she wrote another long note. When she did this, she created the very best piece of evidence she could have left.

Patsy was probably going back down to the basement in a panic, where she probably was feeling a little bit of a heartbeat or even some slight movement from JonBenet.

In desperation, she probably looked for the most readily available items, and that was the stuff in her painting tote. She grabbed her paintbrush and broke it off so she would have a garrote and took some cord that she put around JonBenet's throat.

More than likely she choked JonBenet from behind so she wouldn't have to look at her in the face. JonBenet with that horrible head injury probably did not feel anything.

Then she kept staging the area more to make it look like a kidnapping. JonBenet' wrists were in front of her and not behind her. There were 15 inches of rope between the two arms, and that would have never been able to restrain a small child. In the last minute effort to make it appear that the child had been bound up.

 Then Patsy decided to place a piece of duct tape on JonBenet's mouth. In the forensic lab, they found bloody mucus on the sticky side of the tape, and a perfect set of little child's lip prints. It let detectives know that JonBenet was alive when was placed in her mouth.

He also felt it was off that Patsy was wearing the same clothes from the night before. Patsy was someone who that always thought you needed to look good and she kept a closet full of all the designer clothes. So to Thomas, he was skeptical that she got up and put on the same clothes again.

Three days before the murder there was a call placed from the Ramsey's to 911. The call is cut off before a dispatcher could get to it. Six minutes later, the police called the Ramseys but got voice mail, so a policeman was sent to their home. There were so many people there because there was a Christmas party going on. Anyone could have placed that call.

Two nights later everyone who was anyone was at the Fleet White's Christmas Party. John Ramseys net worth at that time was $6.2 million.

Today, John Ramsey cannot find a job; most companies do not want him because his name is tainted and he says he has sold everything. His large homes, his two planes, his boats, his company and ran out of his retirement savings. He has learned to live by down-sizing.

What was strange was the fact that John Ramsey called the bank and had the $118,000 made available, but did not go pick it up even though the ransom note said if they got the money early, they could have JonBenet back quicker. Why did he not get it to be ready when the kidnappers called?

By 1:00 p.m. that day, no call had come in from the kidnappers. One of the Detectives asked John Ramsey, Fernie, and Fleet White to search the house and check for any signs of JonBenet or if anything that might be missing that could have belonged to JonBenet.

John Ramsey went straight to the basement with the men. Within minutes, Fleet ran back up the stairs, grabbed the phone and yelled for someone to call an ambulance.

One of the Detectives ran to the basement door. John was carrying a little girl in his arms. Her lips were blue, and it looked like she had livor mortis on the back of her body, and she was already in rigor mortis.

She was not breathing, and she was cool to the touch, she already had the odor of decay.

John Ramsey told the Detective he had found her in the wine cellar under a blanket. He had taken some duct tape off her mouth before he brought her upstairs.

Fingers quickly pointed at John Ramsey. A search warrant was acquired, and that is the means by which the body left the house.

Within hours of the finding the body, John Ramsey had made contact with attorneys.

He had contact with high power lawyers to for both he and Patsy.

It has been perceived that things deteriorated between the Boulder Police and the Ramseys so fast were because there had been a leak that the police had asked that the coroner keep the body until Patsy and John agreed to be interrogated by Boulder Police. Detective Thomas denies to this day, this never happened.

The Ramsey's all agreed to handwriting samples, hair samples, and blood samples. There was no problem with them giving in to that request.

They did refuse questioning be conducted separately because they wanted to be questioned together, something the police declined to agree to as well.

Initially, the Ramseys said they would do whatever it took to cooperate with the Boulder police so they could find and apprehend the murderer of JonBenet. But, they kept erecting all kinds of barriers that would stall the investigation forever.

They immediately moved back to Atlanta, Georgia making them hard to get to by Boulder Police. They also offered a $100,000 reward for information that would lead them to the person responsible for JonBenet's death.

Police flew down to Atlanta to interview John Ramsey's son and daughter by his previous marriage as well as his ex-wife, John hired attorneys for all of them.

Since no one had been charged with the crime, the attorneys could not see what evidence the police had.

The Ramsey's for sure would not talk to the police, but they didn't mind talking to CNN January 1, 1997. That is like six days after JonBenet's body was found. In their shoes, I am not sure I could have gone public and discussed the subject. The wounds would still be so fresh.

What this appearance on CNN was about was to influence public opinion. They had hired a firm from Washington to deal with the media.

Of note here: in his interview when John talks about the one room in the basement and turning on the lights because it has no windows. It is important to know that earlier in the day; John had told Police that the door was painted shut.

There were also reports that Fleet White was discouraged by John to not look in that room either. Now Thomas says that Fleet did look into the wine cellar but did not see anything, but he did not know the light switches were outside of the room itself.

Police were also suspicious of the way John acted when he carried JonBenet upstairs. There was no doubt she was dead; she had the odor of decay about her already.

Why did he not call the police downstairs? Why did he not check for signs of life? Why did he lay her on the floor? Why did he not place her on the couch?

Before the body was located, John and Patsy stayed away from each other. Usually, in a situation like this, both parents will be sitting next to each other, clinging to each other for comfort.

When John was coming up the stairs with JonBenet, everyone ran toward him, but not Patsy, she just sat there on the couch.

Thomas was suspicious of Mary Lacy, the sitting District Attorney's involvement with this case. He said he had never known of any sitting District Attorney or prosecutor that had attended the funeral of someone they knew that the Grand Jury were voting to indict criminally, plus travel all across the country to do so. No one could get their arms around that one.

When John Ramsey talks about finding JonBenet's body, he cannot even say "I saw JonBenet" but instead says, "that was her." It seems to allow him to dissociate with the whole incident.

While on CNN Patsy was asked if she felt that JonBenet was in a better place and Patsy made a rambling statement that she will never know the death of a child or never have to no cancer…

Even Patsy couldn't say JonBenet, and her whole attitude just rationalized the situation and was devoid of rage. It seemed she was trying to get the public on board with JonBenet being better off dead, and the fact that her being murdered was just a trivial matter.

When handwriting expert Don Foster at Vassar College analyzed the ransom note, he made some very pointed facts.

Foster said that: *language is infinitely diverse and that no two people use it in quite the same way. They do not have the same vocabulary, use identical spelling and punctuation, construct sentences, in the same manner, read the same books, or express the same beliefs and ideas. Ingrained and unconscious habits are virtually impossible to conceal, even if a writer tries to disguise his identity, he said. Individuals are prisoners of their own language. Foster said the note was written by someone who was trying to deceive.*

Foster also noted that Patsy's handwriting was the only writing samples that changed after the murder. Her entire writing style completely transformed after the killing.

Never let anyone make you think the search stopped at the Ramseys because it did not. It was wide ranging.

1. All employees (former and present) of Access Graphics (and their spouses) – which were 360 employees strong in 1997 – had to give handwriting samples.

2. People who had been at the party at the Ramsey's on the 23rd of December were investigated and questioned.

3. They guy who played Santa for three years straight gave hair, blood and handwriting samples.

4. Santa's wife gave blood, hair and handwriting samples.

The Autopsy

To read the full nine pages of the autopsy report and to look at the autopsy pictures will make you cry.

It states that JonBenet died of ligature strangulation. She had a deep furrow that surrounded her little neck. The skull damage was unbearable. It included an 8-inch long fracture of the skull, with a piece about an inch square that was broken loose and looks like it went inward toward the brain.

What was odd, the scalp had no laceration whatsoever. It seemed more likely that someone had slammed JonBenet's head into a bathtub, a sink, or even against a toilet.

There were abrasions (bruises) on her legs and her back that was probably from being dragged.

There were indicators that she was sexually abused chronically. The Ramsey's dispute this, and so does the family doctor. The medical examiner found not only chronic inflammation in the vaginal tract, but her hymen was opened 1 cm by 1 cm. There were small amounts of blood in her vaginal area and on the crotch of her panties.

Pediatric experts from around the country reviewed this, and all concluded that the trauma in her hymen and the chronic vaginal inflammation were the evidence of both acute and chronic sexual abuse.

When the autopsy findings became public, the world again became a crazy place.

Posters started popping up that said $100,000 reward for the murdered John Ramsey.

Someone by the name of James Michael Thompson stole two pages out of the Boulder morgue, and one of the pages just happened to have JonBenet's name on it. He was later arrested for arson by shoving burning papers through the mail slot of the Ramsey home.

A private investigator and photo lab employee were charged for selling morgue pictures of JonBenet to the tabloid *Globe*. When local supermarkets would not sell the *Globe* issue that had the pictures in it, a local newspaper gave it away for free!

In February 1997, *National Enquirer* reporter, the David Duffy, his body found in his Boulder hotel room. He was covering the JonBenet murder case. His death ruled due to natural causes; there remained persistent rumors of possible foul play.

In the actual autopsy report, there are so many descriptions of bruises all over this child that it is unbearable to let it sink into your mind.

Listed below comes directly from the final autopsy report from the Boulder County Coroner:

1. *Ligature strangulation*

    a. *Circumferential ligature with associated ligature furrow of neck*

    b. *Abrasions and petechial hemorrhages, neck*

    c. *Petechial hemorrhages, conjunctival surfaces of eyes and skin of face*

2. *Craniocerebral injuries*

a. Scalp contusion

b. Linear, comminuted fracture of right side of skull

c. Linear pattern of contusions of right cerebral hemisphere

d. Subarachnoid and subdural hemorrhage

e. Small contusions, tips of temporal lobes

3. Abrasion of right cheek

4. Abrasion/contusion, posterior right shoulder

5. Abrasions of left lower back and posterior left lower leg

6. Abrasion and vascular congestion of vaginal mucosa

7. Ligature of right wrist

*Clinicopathologic Correlation: Cause of the death
of this six-year-old female is asphyxia by
strangulation associated with craniocerebral
trauma.*

And sadly enough, I think this is where we
should end this chapter.

Patsy's Death

It was coming to a close. Patsy's battle with ovarian cancer. Surely everything that had gone on with JonBenet's murder had not helped in any way.

Patsy was getting too weak even to walk, but she got up enough strength for one final task she wanted to complete. She loved painting, and she wanted to finish something for her first exhibit at a soon to be art fair.

Her art teacher came over to Patsy's house, and they stayed up until 11:00 p.m. working to finish the painting. It was of two children on the beach. She said it was Burke and JonBenet. She never said a lot about it, just the fact that it was the two of them.

Her ovarian cancer that had been in remission for nine years, and it recurred in 2002, and her health was on a downhill course. She died with John Ramsey, her husband at her side. It was one battle that she was not going to win.

Her friends will remember her as having the guts and being a graceful southern woman. She was no quitter and she always just kept putting one foot in front of the other. Her legacy was a queen, Miss West Virginia, who put JonBenet, her daughter into the beauty pageant circuits.

She never got away from suspicion of being the one who killed JonBenet. Patsy told PEOPLE magazine that dealing with JonBenet's death

was the worst thing she had ever been through in her life. It makes cancer nothing.

To get away from all the media, John, Patsy and their son Burke moved to Michigan in 2003 and were able to live pretty normal lives. Her friends say it was Patsy's, Christian faith that got her through all the hard times. She stated that this was just our earthly home and heaven is when we will be home.

Patsy's body is interred next to JonBenet's in Atlanta, Georgia.

But How About Burke Now?

Burke is grown now and 30 years old. He works from home and is a software developer. His father says he has recently had a girlfriend but has not found the right one to settle down with him.

What he remembers from Christmas 1996 is that that the last time he saw his sister was Christmas night when she had fallen asleep in the car on the way home from the White's Christmas party.

Burke does not remember hearing any sounds the night she was murdered.

The first thing that he does remember is his mother bursting into his room on December 26 and saying something like, 'Oh, my gosh, oh, my gosh,' and she was running around his room wanting to know where JonBenet was?

Burke said into his room came a police officer later shining a flashlight around. Burke states that he just stayed in his bed because he was not for sure what was going on but he felt safer staying there.

Burke said he had rather avoid conflict and he had rather not know what is going on. He did say that eventually he went down to the kitchen area and there were other people down there. He found out from detectives that his sister was missing.

When the investigators said she was missing, Burke told them she was just probably hiding somewhere. He asked them if they had checked the whole house and had they checked outside?

He said later he was taken to a friend's house where eventually his dad came to him and told him about JonBenet's death. John Ramsey said she was in heaven. Burke said he started crying and at first, he didn't believe his dad.

After he had been on the Dr. Phil show and critics were giving Burke a hard time, Dr. Phil sprang to his defense. He told people that he had spent time with Burke and he was a nice, young man.

He was just very anxious. It was all a matter of being uncomfortable socially. There was nothing creepy or weird about him. He was just nervous.

Burke says he resents whoever killed his sister. Whoever murdered her has messed up my life and my family's life.

Dr. Phil, in the interview, asked Burke if John and Patsy were covering up a murder to protect him, Burke? Burke told Dr. Phil that he didn't know how to answer that one, because, he, Burke knew that is not what happened.

Burke said he always felt like it was a pedophile who probably had seen her in one of the beauty pageants and snuck into our house.

Dr. Phil suggested asked if it was possible for someone to sneak into their house during the holiday home tour and hide out. Burke told him he guessed it was possible; he had just never thought about it.

There is an expert by the name of Werner Spitz, who is known the world over as an authority on death and its causes. He was involved in the investigation in 1996.

Dr. Spitz says it was the boy who did it, whether he was mentally unfit, or jealous or something else because I am no psychiatrist, but I know it was him and he killed her. His parents changed the whole scene to make it look like something it never was.

Burke will tell you that he avoids social events because since his sister's murder, their family has been plagued by reporters and investigators, and it has been miserable. He attended an IT school so he could pursue the job he has now and he can work from home and avoid the stares and the reporters, even 20 years later.

Burke came forward to speak to Dr. Phil, no questions barred hoping to put some of the questions to rest. All Burke wants is to be able to get on with his life, to some semblance of a normal life.

What Are John Ramsey's Thoughts Now?

John Ramsey still looks wealthy in the way he carries himself and the way he dresses.

He now lives in Michigan, in a remote town called Charlevoix. He lives in a mustard colored house in the shadow of the mansion where he once lived in the summer time.

He laughs as he sees an old station wagon going by and pulling a motor home. He states that is where he will probably be living next.

John has lost everything he once had, and no one wants to hire him because he invites negative press, so he still does a bit of consulting.

He said he would have to sell Patsy's oversized antiques next. There are many of them.

When John is being asked how all the losses in his life has affected him, he says that they all tear something out of your heart, and that part cannot be repaired.

He went on to say that it takes a total of four or five years just to start to get over it and start to live again. Fear seems to paralyze you. At times you think about suicide because you just do not want to live anymore. You make some bad decisions. He said he would take Benedryl and go to bed at six in the evening.

He said as far as his son, Burke; I don't want anyone to get near him. If anything happened to Burke, I would not survive.

Sometimes I see in a crowd a flash of a little coat on a little girl that looks like JonBenet... and I can't bear to hear little children crying; I just can't take it.

John goes every Sunday to a nearby church, just like he did with Patsy. He is obsessed with reading theology books that are everywhere in the sunroom.

Let us think about it this way; four years before JonBenet, Beth, his daughter from his first marriage died in a tragic car accident. Then, shortly after that, Patsy was diagnosed with Stage Four ovarian cancer but delayed giving John the news because he was already grieving.

She went into the hospital for one year for intense treatments that were thought to be successful. Then on December 26, 1996, John finds his JonBenet dead in his home.

Suffering this much tragedy, how could anyone have a typical reaction. John Ramsey's responses to everything was and is still judged. The entire family's reactions were and are still judged. John said they wanted him to cry and wail in front of all of them that morning. John stated that people have no idea how I was feeling.

John was also criticized for hiring a lawyer so quickly. John said that someone inside the law enforcement system called him the second day and told him he better get an attorney because they were already targeting John as the prime suspect.

John felt like where things began to fall apart was when a rookie cop answered the 911 call, and she had no experience in kidnapping cases that she did not even seal off our house or collect any evidence.

She even sent someone back to get the book on kidnapping so she would know what to do. Later they took 200 DNA samples, and supposedly they eliminated our friends and acquaintances so they could look at the only ones that they thought had killed JonBenet and that was us. And, none of the Ramsey's DNA was found on her body.

The police started fake rumors about the footprints around the house in the snow, and there was no snow that day.

The tabloids followed them no matter where they went. They would bang on their car and call them child killers. They printed up all kinds of garbage about us. There was a Japanese camera crew that broke into Burke's school.

John Ramsey feels he is responsible for JonBenet's death. He thinks his daughter was killed to punish him.

Just a few days before she died, John's company ran an article profiling its record-breaking billion dollars sales. John says he regrets publicizing this information because it drew attention to his family.

He said if he could do things over there are two things he would have done differently. One would be to live in a very secure home. Second, blend in with the crowd. If your head rises above everyone else, there are people who will target you.

There are some who even question why they put JonBenet's date of death as December 25th on her tombstone. REALLY? People, knock it off! The coroner determined the time of death.

Geraldo Rivera was stupid enough to broadcast a mock trial of the Ramseys. Geraldo and his ratings, he cares for no one but himself, he is so ego driven. Geraldo

Rivera's stunt alone caused them to take all the TV sets out of their house, and they canceled their newspapers. Burke had to see a child psychologist for two years.

One of Patsy's friends, Pam Archuleta, told that Patsy became obsessed by the pageants for JonBenet. Patsy had all her costumes hand made in New York. She took her to have her highlighted and to piano lessons and singing lessons.

John, himself did not like the cost of the costumes and the whole pageant mess. Archuleta said that he and Patsy argued about it.

There were even times Patsy doubted herself about what effect it may have on JonBenet. She is just too friendly with people and she flirts with them is what she told Pam and Pam's husband.

Some of their close friends felt that JonBenet's bedwetting was some protest against the pageants. But JonBenet still acted like an adult for half of her 5 ½ years.

The last time the Ramseys would be in Boulder was two years after the murder, when the grand jury was going to give its verdict.

John and Patsy had decided if they were to be indicted they would go to turn themselves in, but of course, the press found out about it, and they had to hide at the Archuleta's ranch house.

They were in Atlanta and flew their plane to Chattanooga, Tennessee and then on to Erie Air Park outside the town of Boulder. So Archuleta borrowed a beat up Volvo, and they drove to her dentist's parking lot and got into her Audi. They laid down in her back seat so no one would see them.

Archuleta said that the first night she could hear Patsy sobbing and she went in and gathered Patsy in a hug. She had gotten so small and thin. She was shriveled and pale, and Archuleta knew the cancer was coming back.

When they knew the verdict was coming, they were in the front of the television and Patsy wanted them to all hold hands, kneel down and pray. Then when they announced 'no indictment' Patsy was her old self again.

John and Patsy were no longer welcome in Boulder, so they went quickly back to Atlanta. Behind them, they left a string of damaged lives and ruined friendships.

One couple who was their best friends turned against them when the wife started to suspect it was Patsy. The local radio stations became virulent in their accusations. If they could have hung the Ramseys, they would have.

It caused so much mess in that town it was hard to believe. People lost their jobs when they sided for the Ramseys'. Two families had to go into seclusion; one woman went into complete seclusion; another woman just disappeared into thin air.

A famous restaurant owner in Boulder went to jail when he wielded a metal pipe at a reporter. One couple quit their jobs, moved to Atlanta, and wound up without jobs there when John's new business failed. Pam Archuleta lost her marriage.

For a very brief time, after Patsy died, John dated Beth Twitty, Natalee Holloway's mother, the girl who disappeared in Aruba. He says she is a beautiful lady and they went their different ways because Beth was behind him in the area of her grief cycle.

John is moving on with life though. He has remarried and is heading up a promotional marketing company out in Las Vegas. His new wife, a fashion designer, Jan Rousseau, is 54.

They got married in front of a party of 60 guests that included her two grown children and John's three grown children. Jan said that John has got the most confidence of any anyone I have ever met and the least ego.

But there was nothing to prepare her for the day she went to pick up John's wedding ring. The guy behind the counter said that Ramsey's son did it. Jan told him the son was only nine years old. The man would not shut up and told Jan that the family knows what happened and they're just not telling. Jan said he was wrong and walked out of the store.

John says of 1996 that the worst moment was when she was missing, not when he found her because when he found her, she was cradled back in his arms.

John said when Burke reached high school, they decided to move to Charlevoix, Michigan and to make his life as normal as they could. But, at 19 years old, Burke lost his mother, Patsy. John says that Burke is a pretty quiet guy and has a job in the high-tech world. Burke has a 401(K) plan and an IRA, and he has done it all on his own.

John is still suspicious that one of their close friends with access to their house had some role in JonBenet's murder, and to this day he questions that person's alibi. Their friend Michael Archuleta, who was the pilot for John shares the same suspicion.

The Ramseys reportedly sued CBS, for airing "The Case of JonBenet Ramsey" that aired on their network and was full of unprofessional television attacks and false revelations for alleging that Burke could be the killer in the still unsolved murder.

Wood, their attorney, said that the lawsuit was to be filed on behalf of Burke. He went on to say that CBS's attacks on Burke were revolting and disgusting. He alleged that CBS is made up of nothing but 'profit mongers' and stated that the documentary was full of nothing but omissions, distortions, misrepresentations, and lies.'

How About the Private Investigator?

Remember, the Ramseys hired their personal investigator, Ollie Gray, outside and away from the police and the FBI. Someone who would be looking out for their interests. Not for the benefit of the fake news and the tabloids.

Ollie Gray had a lot to say, but for some reason, the Boulder Police nor the FBI would listen to him.

Ollie claims it was a local boy, 26 years old and his family owned a junkyard at the edge of Boulder. His name was Michael Helgoth.

Ollie feels that based on everything that he knows now, that Helgoth had accomplices and committed the crime. His opinion is backed up by a man by the name of John

Kenady who used to work for Helgoth. Kenady stated that there is a tape somewhere and someone has it that states that he is the one who killed JonBenet.

Kenady claims that he knew something was up a month before the murder.

Helgoth was bragging that he and a partner were getting ready to come into some cash, and each of them would be getting around $50,000 or $60,000.   Kenady said he would never forget one day when they were walking toward Helgoth's house, and he said he just wondered what it would be like to crack a human skull.

Gray was frustrated because he had left 20 messages for them to interview Helgoth and they did not. Kenady provided relevant information for the case that should have taken priority, but it went nowhere.

It seemed that all Boulder police could think about was hanging John and Patsy Ramsey for the murder.

Helgoth died from what looked like an apparent suicide at his home. But Kenady believes he was killed by one of the other accomplices because the Helgoth's gun was found on his right side, but the bullet hole entry point was from the left side. Ollie thinks he was murdered to keep his mouth shut.

Helgoth was cleared of the killing when his DNA did not match that found under the fingernails of JonBenet. And, since we do not know who the accomplices were, we can't test them now, can we?

Ollie Gray still thinks that Helgoth was the killer, and he could tell the police how to solve this case once and for all, but they do not want to listen to him.

Close

Two decades later and still no real answer to who the murderer or murderers were in this case.

We can be sure that there were many, many tabloids who made a fortune off the misfortune of a tiny child. There were many lawyers who made enough money to retire from that same misfortune. That in itself is a tragedy. How low some will stoop for money is beyond me.

There are so many possibilities to look at that it all gets so confusing.

I cannot imagine what the family was put through, how others treated them. I have had my suspicions all along, and I still hold fast to them today. If my suspicions are correct, they will never be known, and this murder will never be solved.

Not having all the information that the police have packed away and the information they should have had packed away that they overlooked and missed that first day was difficult to give an educated guess.

However, from the information, we do know from retired detectives and autopsy reports, and those who were there during those first few hours, it does help us have a pretty good idea as to what probably happened.

I cannot imagine the suffering that little girl went through. I can only hope that the cracked and damaged skull did not cause her to suffer long, that it was instant coma for her and that she did not feel anything else that happened to her. I try not to think of the pain she must have suffered from her head wound until she was unconscious.

For those who say she had not been chronically sexually abused, they need to read the autopsy reports again and the reviews of all the pediatricians across the country. I would still like to know that answer.

I, in my heart, do not think it was by anyone in the home that had anything to do with the chronic molestation. The person responsible for this act should be found and then be left to rot in hell. JonBenet was suffering long before she died and only one person knew it.

I know her Pediatrician vehemently denied that she had been chronically sexually abused. Her pediatrician would have had no way of knowing this for certain unless he specifically examined her for that purpose. I seriously doubt that he performed that test on a child of her age and of her family's status.

It is my opinion alone, but I feel that we have two crimes. One of chronic rape and one of murder. JonBenet did not deserve either; she deserved a chance at life.

Printed in Great Britain
by Amazon